EN

Edited by
CLIVE BATTY

CARLTON
BOOKS

First published by Carlton Books in 2006

This book is not an officially licensed product of the
Football Association

Text and design copyright © Carlton Books Limited 2006

A CIP catalogue record for this book is available
from the British library.

ISBN 1 84442 250 X

Printed in Singapore

INTRODUCTION

Thirty years of hurt? Make that forty... and counting. Yes, England fans have been put through the wringer since that glorious day back in 1966 when Bobby Moore proudly held aloft the World Cup trophy at Wembley. True, there have been moments when another great English triumph has appeared imminent – but they've all ended in tears. Usually after a stomach-churning penalty shoot-out.

Those gripping, edge-of-the-seat encounters at World Cups and European Championships loom large in this collection of bite-sized quotes about the England team. Players, managers, opponents, pundits and fans all have their say with comments which range from the inspired to the inane, the profound to the perplexing. Much the same sort of mixture, in fact, that England's finest specialise in serving up on the pitch.

❝In England winning at football is treated like winning a battle... the English nationalism is more than football.❞

German TV commentator **Werner Schneider**

"I read it in the papers every World Cup that this will be England's year. They won't win, just like Tim Henman never wins the Wimbledon title."

George Best, 2005

❛At Wembley it got warmer and warmer as you went up the tunnel and what hit you, apart from the noise, was the smell of fried onions.**❜**

England striker *Malcolm Macdonald* recalls the old Wembley atmosphere

'I'm nervous about meeting so many new people. It's like when you go out with a woman for the first time – you're bound to wonder how it will end up.**'**

Sven-Goran Eriksson
before his first England game, 2001

❝I want more from David Beckham. I want him to improve on perfection.**❞**

Kevin Keegan, 2000

❝Lord Nelson, Lord Beaverbrook, Sir Winston Churchill, Sir Anthony Eden, Clement Attlee, Henry Cooper, Lady Diana, Maggie Thatcher. Can you hear me? Your boys took a helluva beating. Norway has beaten England at football.❞

Norwegian TV commentator **Burge Lillelien**, 1981

❛In the studio, Des Lynam's line-up of pundits resembled an evolutionary wall-chart of human articulacy, starting with Paul Gascoigne at the primeval end and peaking, surprisingly, with Gary Neville.**❜**

Mail on Sunday TV critic **David Bennun**
on ITV's coverage of England-Denmark, 2002

"After six weeks in the England camp, even Jack Charlton could look attractive."

England 1966 World Cup winner *George Cohen*

❝You've beaten them once. Now go out and bloody beat them again.**❞**

Alf Ramsey to his England team at
the start of extra-time in the 1966 World Cup final

"A little bit the hand of God, a little the head of Diego."

Diego Maradona describes his first goal against England at the 1986 World Cup

> It wasn't the hand of God. It was the hand of a rascal. God had nothing to do with it.

England manager **Bobby Robson** rejects
the notion of divine intervention
in Maradona's goal

'England, especially forward, astonished the spectators by some very pretty dribbling, an art curious and novel.'

Report in the **North British Mail** of the first England-Scotland match, 1872

> **'**The worst moment of my life was giving the Nazi salute in Berlin in 1938. I felt a fool heiling Hitler, but we went out determined to beat the Germans.**'**

Former England captain *Eddie Hapgood*.
England won the match 6–3.

If you are a Swede who has lived in Portugal and Italy, you don't know very much about cricket. It is a great sport in England but in Sweden we never play it.

Sven-Goran Eriksson fails to get caught up in Ashes fever, 2005

'You look round and think, "I remember watching them on the telly – they're England." And you don't feel as if you should be here with them.'

Chris Waddle, 1990

‘I still cringe when I look back on that game and I take absolutely no satisfaction whatsoever in being able to say I took part in the soccer sensation of the century.’

Tom Finney on England's shock defeat by the USA in the 1950 World Cup

❛The Hungarians produced some of the finest, most brilliantly applied football it has ever been my privilege to see. The ball did precisely what they wanted. They were relentless. They were superb.❜

Billy Wright after Hungary beat England 6–3 at Wembley in 1953

❝No one cares whether you win or lose. There seems to be more animation on a PlayStation.❞

Former skipper **Terry Butcher** is not a fan of modern England friendlies

‘Because of the booking
I will miss the Holland
game – if selected.’

Paul Gascoigne, 1993

" Never, in any other match, have I been kicked when the ball was at the other end. I'd look round and one of their fellows would make a gesture of innocence. It was the worst behaviour I've ever experienced. "

Roger Hunt on the England-Argentina
World Cup clash, 1966

'England's best football will come against the right type of opposition – a team who come to play football and not act as animals.'

Alf Ramsey, reacting angrily to foul play by Argentina in the same match

‘It was not a goal, because the ball bounced down and hit the line. That's no goal, you know, the whole ball has to be behind the line. That's the rule.’

West Germany's *Franz Beckenbauer* disputes the validity of England's third goal in the 1966 World Cup final

'I have to admit that I had a bit of sympathy for the Germans. They genuinely believed the ball had not crossed the line and they may be right.'

Scorer **Geoff Hurst** isn't completely sure it was a goal, either – but hey, who cares, we won!

"I don't remember anyone making such an impact on a tournament since Pele in the 1958 World Cup."

Sven-Goran Eriksson talks up
Wayne Rooney at Euro 2004

> ❛I've heard he's being compared with Pele, but I personally think he's the best talent since Maradona because I thought Maradona had a better all-round game than Pele.❜

Former Everton youth coach
Colin Harvey on Rooney, 2004

> As we came round the corner from the 18th green, a crowd of members were at the clubhouse window, cheering and waiting to tell me that England had won the World Cup. It was the blackest day of my life.

Scotland striker **Denis Law**, 1979

❝I could see Colin Hendry coming in, so I flicked it over his head and volleyed it. God, the feeling when I scored was magnificent! I'm so glad I scored that goal.❞

Paul Gascoigne on his famous goal against Scotland at Euro 96

'We owe the English big time. They stole our land, our oil, perpetrated the Highland Clearances and now they've even pinched Billy Connolly.'

Gordon Strachan before the Euro 2000 play-off between England and Scotland

‘There was a lot made of the patriotism of the Scots, the whole *Braveheart* thing, and I remember thinking, "Don't you understand we're patriots, too? How much it means for me to play for my country?"’

Gareth Southgate on the England-Scotland meeting at Euro 96

> **❝**Back home, they'll be
> thinking about us
> When we are far away
> Back home, they'll be really behind us
> In every game we play...**❞**

England 1970 World Cup squad,
singing their chart-topping
single 'Back Home'

‘After the match I had to do a drugs test, but I'd lost so much fluid that I couldn't give a urine sample. I'd lost a stone in weight and I had to drink eight bottles of Coke before I could give them something. ’

Alan Mullery's postscript to the England-Brazil game, 1970

'What chance has any other top striker got with England while old golden boy Shearer is still on the scene? It's an issue which bugs me.'

Andy Cole, 1999

"England have the best fans in the world and Scotland's fans are second to none."

Kevin Keegan, 1999

❛At that moment I hated Gordon Banks more than any man in soccer. But when I cooled down I had to applaud him with my heart for the greatest save I had ever seen.**❜**

Pele after Banks had saved his header in the 1970 World Cup match between England and Brazil

❛I still get excited when I see the save on TV; it's been shown so many times, and of course it's nice when people talk about it as the greatest save ever.**❜**

Gordon Banks, 1997

'Afterwards we were devastated. With a bad defeat in the League it might last for a couple of days, but this was something completely different. It stayed with me for weeks; it was terrible.'

Colin Bell on England's failure to qualify for the 1974 World Cup

‘It's worse than losing a war, a national crisis of the highest magnitude.’

Lord George Wigg speaks for the nation
on the same subject, 1973

> **I'm the man for the job. I can revive our World Cup hopes. I couldn't do a worse job, could I?**

Monster Raving Loony Party leader
Screaming Lord Sutch puts his name in the
frame for the England manager's job, 1994

❛Michael Owen – he's got the legs of a salmon.**❜**

Former Scotland manager *Craig Brown*

❝ I made the first move. They did not contact me. I fancied being England manager. **❞**

Don Revie on his appointment as England boss in 1975

'As soon as it dawned on me that we were short of players who combined skill and commitment, I should have forgotten all about trying to play more controlled, attractive football and settled for a real bastard of a team.'

Don Revie after resigning as England manager, 1977

'This Eriksson bloke must be the fat cat of international football, living out his nine lives. How he's got the gall to stay in his job, raking in £4million a year, beats me.'

Brian Clough, 2004

'Sven's attitude towards the England job has stunk for ages. To have contact with Manchester United and Chelsea about becoming their next manager while leading the country is wrong. It shows his mind is elsewhere.'

Jimmy Greaves, 2005

'Don Revie's decision doesn't surprise me in the slightest. Now I only hope he can quickly learn how to call out bingo numbers in Arabic.'

Football League secretary **Alan Hardaker** after Revie, who was famous for organizing his players' leisure time, left the England job to manage in the United Arab Emirates

"A sensational, outrageous example of disloyalty, breach of duty, discourtesy and selfishness."

Mr Justice Cantley QC accuses Revie of bringing the game into disrepute in a court case that resulted, 1979

❝Whether you are white, brown, purple or blue, it's the same. When you are fortunate enough to make an England debut at Wembley, it's the greatest feeling in the world.**❞**

Viv Anderson, the first black player to be capped by England

❝I worked for the last three England managers and I saw what it could do to them. I saw Ron Greenwood break out in sores.**❞**

Howard Wilkinson, some years before he became England caretaker manager in 2000

> **❝**I loved the goal, of course, but it created many problems for me, particularly in changing perceptions. After scoring a goal like that, I never lived up to England's expectations again.**❞**

John Barnes on his famous solo dribble
against Brazil in 1984

"Why couldn't John Barnes play for England the way he played for Liverpool? If he was a chicken winger I could have understood it, but we are talking about a brave man, built like a cruiserweight boxer."

Bobby Robson

England are always a tough team. When you have someone like Michael Owen, who can score out of nowhere, and David Beckham, who can win you a game at any time with one of his free-kicks, you always have a chance.

Thierry Henry, 2004

❝I have to be honest and say that I felt Bobby Robson was a bit bumbling at times. When I first turned up for training, he called me Paul Adams.**❞**

Tony Adams, 1998

> *Catch me if you can*
> *Cos I'm the England man*
> *And what you're looking at*
> *Is the masterplan*

John Barnes rapping on 'World in Motion',
England's 1990 World Cup song with New Order

❛You people provide the pressure. If you people didn't exist, my job would be twice as easy and twice as pleasurable.**❜**

Bobby Robson to the England press pack, 1985

'When I was shown the yellow card I knew my World Cup had come to an end. When things are good and I can see they're about to end I get scared, really scared. I couldn't help but cry that night.'

Paul Gascoigne recalls his tearful outburst against Germany in 1990

'Neil Webb threw me a towel
because I was sobbing my heart out.
I had it over my head like a
convicted criminal leaving
a courthouse.**'**

Stuart Pearce on his reaction to England's penalty
shoot-out defeat by Germany in 1990

'Shearer could be at 100 per cent fitness, but not peak fitness.**'**

England manager *Graham Taylor*

❝ Hitler didn't tell us when he was going to send over those doodlebugs, did he? **❞**

Bobby Robson refuses to name his
England team in advance of an international game, 1989

‘Swedes 2, Turnips 1’

Headline in *The Sun* after Graham Taylor's
England lost to Sweden in 1992

❛I used to quite like turnips. Now my wife refuses to serve them.**❜**

Graham Taylor, 1995

'In the name of Allah, go!'

The Sun calls for Bobby Robson to quit as manager after England drew with Saudi Arabia, 1988

'Yanks 2, Planks 0'

Headline in **The Sun** after England lost to USA, 1993

> **❝** He'll flick one. Koeman's going to flick this. Goal! **❞**

Brian Moore, commentating on the Holland-England match in 1993. Koeman scored the winning goal after he should have been sent off

❝ I'm just saying to your colleague, the referee's got me the sack. Thank him ever so much for that, won't you? **❞**

Graham Taylor confronts a FIFA official and linesman during the same game

"It was a clear foul, the keeper was in his own area and must be protected. England are looking for a scapegoat and they are looking to blame me."

Referee **Urs Meier**, explaining why he disallowed Sol Campbell's goal against Portugal at Euro 2004

The way some of the English press have blamed Urs Meier after a correct decision is completely unacceptable. To go into his private life, to show his wife, his car and put an England flag on his home is unacceptable.

UEFA referees' committee president
Volker Roth, 2004

'That's football, Mike. Northern Ireland have had several chances and haven't scored, but England have had no chances and scored twice.'

Trevor Brooking, commentating on a Euro 1988 qualifier

'Poland nil, England nil, though England are looking the better value for their nil.'

Barry Davies, commentating on a Euro 2000 qualifier

"With Gazza around, you can expect to get pepper in your dessert and it has been known for him to book a sun-bed for one of the black players in the squad."

Dennis Wise on England team-mate Paul Gascoigne

'We used to sing 'Three Lions', the Skinner and Baddiel song, for a laugh on the team coach. Gazza had it blaring out of his room at all hours of the day and night.'

Robbie Fowler on England's Euro 96 preparations

'Leading out the England team, it felt like Wembley was my ground; the night, everything, belonged to me.'

David Platt on captaining England for the first time in 1993

"There are two ways of getting the ball. One is from your own team-mates, and that's the only way."

England manager Terry Venables

❝I only went in for a filling and I came out drunk – it must have been some anaesthetic! But get the video tapes of that tournament and you'll see how successful the dentist's chair was!❞

Paul Gascoigne, recalling an infamous England squad drinking session prior to Euro 96

❝I've been asked that question for the last six months. It is not fair to expect me to make such a fast decision on something that has been put upon me like that.**❞**

Terry Venables on whether he would remain England manager after Euro 96

'It's a piece of our history. I never thought I'd see it again.**'**

Geoff Hurst after being reunited with the
1966 World Cup final ball 30 years on

> *Three lions on a shirt
> Jules Rimet still gleaming
> Thirty years of hurt
> Never stopped me dreaming*

Baddiel and Skinner with The Lightning Seeds on England's Euro 96 song, 'Three Lions'

❝I've always said that I would love to play not just in this World Cup but the one in South Africa too. But we'll have to wait and see about that. We'll have to see how my legs are!❞

David Beckham, 2005

"Wait until you come to Turkey" was the shout, with fingers being passed across throats. And that was just the kit man!

Gareth Southgate on Turkish reaction to an England victory in 2003

'When we're away on holiday he obviously still thinks about what he's going to do because he doodles attack plans on napkins. All our newspapers are covered in crosses and arrows. '

Yvette Venables, wife of England manager Terry, 1995

‘Football is a simple game. The hard part is making it look simple.’

England manager **Ron Greenwood**, 1978

I put the penalty where I wanted but not far enough in the corner. When he saved it, there was just an incredible sense of deflation, a sense of: this really wasn't meant to happen.

Gareth Southgate, recalling his Euro 96 penalty miss against Germany

‘Why didn't you just belt it, son?’

Barbara Southgate, Gareth's mother,
speaks for the nation, 1996

'I knew I wasn't going to the World Cup, so I stormed into Glenn's room and kicked the door down. Phil Neville came running out and I just started calling Glenn all the names under the sun.'

Paul Gascoigne on his omission from Glenn Hoddle's England squad for the 1998 World Cup

'Seventy-five per cent of what happens to Paul Gascoigne in his life is fiction.'

Glenn Hoddle, attempting to play down newspaper reports of the incident

The missing of chances is one of the mysteries of life.

Sir Alf Ramsey, England manager, 1972

The nice aspect of football captaincy is that the manager gets the blame if things go wrong.

Gary Lineker on being made England captain, 1990

❛Michael Owen is a goalscorer –
not a natural born one, not yet,
that takes time.❜

Glenn Hoddle, speaking at the 1998 World Cup

❝David Beckham is the only British player who would get into the Brazilian squad.❞

Rivaldo, Brazilian World Cup star

❝There's one thing I can say without fear of contradiction: I know I couldn't have buried it any better.❞

Michael Owen on his famous goal against Argentina at the 1998 World Cup

If Glenn Hoddle said one word to his team at half-time, it was concentration and focus.

Ron Atkinson, commentating on
England-Argentina, 1998

'At the time it was really special, especially against the old enemy. In Scotland they try to erase the game from the memory; if you tried to talk about it they'd change the subject.'

Jimmy Armfield on England's 9–3 victory
over Scotland in 1961

> **❝**Everywhere I went people would shout at me, "What time is it, Frank? Nine past Haffey."**❞**

Frank Haffey, Scotland's goalkeeper on the same game

‟David Beckham's sending-off cost us dearly. It was a mistake. But these things happen in football. I am not denying it cost us the game.„

Glenn Hoddle on England's World Cup defeat by Argentina, 1998

'Beckham's silly little, smart little kick at his Argentinian opponent was what is wrong with the national character.'

Leader in *The Daily Telegraph*, 1998

'They came at us playing direct football. They were more English than the English.'

Graham Taylor after England lost to Sweden in 1992

England will never win World Cups. We simply don't have enough people who believe in playing football.

Alex Ferguson, 1995

'Mary and I got the shock of our lives when David was asked to take a penalty. Neither of us really expected David to score.'

Al Batty, David's father, on his son's penalty miss against Argentina in 1998

It was only when I got back to the hotel, in the peace of my room, that I realized, "My God, we were so close."

Terry Butcher, reflecting on England's 1990 World Cup semi-final defeat by Germany

❝You and I have been physically given two hands and two legs and half-decent brains. Some people have not been born like that for a reason; karma is working from another lifetime.**❞**

Glenn Hoddle's comments on the disabled which led to his resignation as England manager, 1999

❛ Hoddle's attitude betrays a disabled mind. It seems he has no compassion, no allowance for weakness. **❜**

Ian Dury, singer and actor, 1999

❝Napoleon wanted his generals to be lucky. I don't think he would have worked with me.**❞**

Graham Taylor after England failed to reach the 1994 World Cup

❝That man could talk and talk and talk until the cows came home and he'd continue talking until they were fast asleep. The problem was most of it didn't make any sense to me.**❞**

Ian Wright on Graham Taylor's England team talks

It's ironic that it's left to me to save the England team when no one will let me have a UK passport.

Fulham owner *Mohamed Al Fayed* after agreeing to let Kevin Keegan become England manager, 1999

❝Tony Blair is very good-looking but unfortunately he has no bravado. Same with the England football team. They play so slow.❞

Adriana Sklenarikova,
Slovakian Wonderbra model, 2000

❝I can't say England are shite because they beat us in the (Euro 2000) play-offs, and that would make us even shittier.**❞**

Former Scotland striker *Ally McCoist*, 2000

❝ England can end the millennium as it started – as the greatest football nation in the world. **❞**

England manager **Kevin Keegan**, 1999

'The Germans only have one player under 22, and he's 23.'

Kevin Keegan on England's Euro 2000 opponents

'Portugal play football as I like to see it played. As a neutral it was fantastic. Unfortunately I'm not a neutral.**'**

Kevin Keegan after Portugal beat England at Euro 2000

"The bottom line is that we were inept tactically, we were exposed against teams we could have beaten. England's failings have nothing to do with technical failings because I don't agree we're not good enough as footballers."

Martin Keown after England's exit at Euro 2000

❝I just feel I fall a little short of what is required in this job. I sat there in the first half and could see things weren't right but I couldn't find it in myself to solve the problem.**❞**

Kevin Keegan, announcing his resignation as England manager, 2000

❝I feel I have broken the ice with the English people. In 60 days, I have gone from being Volvo Man to Svensational.❞

Sven-Goran Eriksson after his first game as England manager, 2001

❝I don't shout, it's just not in my character. I'm not like, say, Giovanni Trappatoni who jumps up and down and shouts and screams throughout every game.**❞**

Sven-Goran Eriksson, 2001

fAt last England have appointed a manager who speaks English better than the players. **J**

Brian Clough, reacting to Sven-Goran Eriksson's appointment, 2001

❛He may look like Mr Burns out of *The Simpsons*... but he's most things we want and need in a man, sooner or later.**❜**

Former *Cosmopolitan* editor **Marcelle d'Argy Smith** on Sven-Goran Eriksson, 2002

"I have no doubts whatsoever that Germany will thrash England and qualify easily for the World Cup. What could possibly go wrong? The English haven't beaten us in Munich for a hundred years."

Former Germany player, *Uli Hoeness*, before England beat Germany 5–1 in 2001

❝We absolutely annihilated England; it was a massacre. We beat them 5–4.**❞**

Bill Shankly recalls a wartime meeting with the Auld Enemy

We all know we've made history tonight. We all know we are part of something special.

Steven Gerrard after England beat Germany 5–1 in 2001

The 5–1 defeat by England was like the explosion of a nuclear bomb. The scars will last for life.

Germany goalkeeper *Oliver Kahn*

‘The Prime Minister pointed out to the Cabinet that nothing was more important to England's World Cup arrangements than the state of David Beckham's foot. ’

Official spokesman for *Tony Blair*, 2002, after Becks' metatarsal injury before the World Cup finals

❝We needed Winston Churchill and we got Iain Duncan Smith.❞

Anonymous England defender on
Sven-Goran Eriksson's half-time
team talk during the England-Brazil game in 2002

‎'We went out with a whimper in the Brazil game. There was no fight. I'd rather you get Martin Keown on and put him up front and go out fighting.'

Steve McManaman on England's 2002 World Cup exit

"It was obvious England were overawed by Brazil, Brazil with 10 players, men against boys. You could see England's body language at the end: "We've done okay, haven't we? Got to the quarter-finals.""

Roy Keane, 2002

❝Some people are on the pitch. They think it's all over... it is now!❞

Kenneth Wolstenholme, commenting on the 1966 World Cup final for the BBC as Geoff Hurst scored England's fourth goal

❝Everybody went crazy, but I wasn't sure if it was a goal because the ref seemed to blow his whistle as the ball went in. When I realized it was a goal I was incredibly pleased.❞

Geoff Hurst, who now has a tendency to finish public speaking engagements with the words, 'They think it's all over... it is now!'

'All the European teams who have gone out played too defensive – like they were scared. I thought England were the worst.'

South Korea coach *Guus Hiddink* on England's World Cup exit, 2002

'There have, of course, been worse moments in English history – the Roman Conquest, the Black Death, the Civil War, the fall of France in 1940 and virtually the whole of the 1970s, for example.'

Leader in *The Times*, putting England's 2002 World Cup failure in perspective

"We were encouraged to open ourselves to the Japanese cuisine on offer, but having been away from home for so long I could have died for a McDonald's."

Danny Mills on the England team's
World Cup diet, 2002

‟I respected Don (Revie) most of all because he was the first manager to make sure England internationals got paid a decent amount of appearance money.„

Stan Bowles, 2004

'At the end of the final I remember being absolutely drained. I've seen some photographs after the game and I look about 90!'

England 1966 World Cup winner **Ray Wilson**

❝ Even now kids come up to me and say, "You're the one who won the World Cup and did that jig with no teeth." **❞**

Nobby Stiles, 2003

‟No one could believe it. Everyone ran up to the referee, I ran up to him... it was just incredible that the goal was given. It's still hard to believe.„

Peter Shilton recalls Maradona's 'Hand of God' goal against England at the 1986 World Cup

❝Malvinas 2, England 1! We blasted the English pirates with Maradona and a little hand. He who robs a thief has a thousand years of pardon.❞

Argentinian newspaper *Cronica*, 1986

❝We were the world champions, which was a fantastic feeling. I knew that life for me would never be the same again.**❞**

Bobby Charlton's reaction to England's 1966 World Cup triumph

‘Let club directors make a hash of the affairs of their own teams, but spare England the catastrophe of their attentions.’

Former England player **Len Shackleton**, 1958

❝As for Maradona's second goal, well that was something special. All I saw was the back of him running, this number ten steaming down the pitch.**❞**

Kenny Sansom on the England-Argentina match at the 1986 World Cup

'The little lad jumped like a salmon and tackled like a ferret. '

Bobby Robson on Paul Parker's performances at the 1990 World Cup

We didn't underestimate them. They were a lot better than we thought.

Bobby Robson on England's 1990 World Cup opponents, Cameroon

❝I remember a milkman asking me just after the 1966 final what it was like to be married to a star. "I don't know," I replied. "I've never been married to one."❞

Judith Hurst, wife of England hat-trick hero Geoff

'Being an ex-England manager, one that failed to qualify for the World Cup, is like being a dead politician.'

Graham Taylor

❝ This side can be the greatest that football has ever had, the greatest football will ever know. **❞**

Sir Alf Ramsey on his England team, 1967

❝The biggest mistake I made was not getting Eileen Drewery out to join us from the start.**❞**

Glenn Hoddle wishes he'd included the faith healer in his 1998 England World Cup squad

'Don't tell me I would have failed as England manager. I'll never believe it for a second. Me? Working with the best of the very best? I couldn't have failed.'

Brian Clough, who was interviewed for the England job in 1977

"So, Gordon, if you were English, what formation would you play?"

"If I was English I'd top myself!"

Gordon Strachan replies to Gary Lineker, 2004

❝It was as if we had beaten a country, more than just a football team.**❞**

Diego Maradona on Argentina's defeat of England in 1986

❝I do want to play the short ball and I do want to play the long ball. I think long and short balls is what football is all about.**❞**

England manager *Bobby Robson*

❝It's amazing what you can see through Sven's specs – I must get a pair.**❞**

Gary Lineker

‘FA chiefs laid down laws about good behaviour before Euro 2004, but now the sex scandal is making the FA's own home look slightly more louche than the Playboy mansion.’

Mirror columnist **Tony Parsons** on the Eriksson, Palios and Faria Alam affair, 2004

‘I am French but I was supporting England. It's my country but I don't want to know about France – I was born there but I feel English.’

Eric Cantona, backing England at Euro 2004

"I've scored four goals a couple of times before, but I don't remember ever scoring five in a game. But 8–0 against Poland has certainly got everyone thinking there could be a few goals about."

Michael Owen looks forward to a goal-fest against Azerbaijan, 2005

‘Who is Michael Owen anyway? What has he ever won in football? This man, this midget, I refuse to talk about him any more.’

Carlos Alberto, coach of Azerbaijan, 2005

'Sven's got to go. Our readers say it. We say it. The sex-crazed Swede has had the benefit of the doubt for far too long. What's he done for English football? Sweet Faria Alam.'

Leader column in *The Sun*, 2005

❝Eriksson should go, because this man has as good a chance of winning the World Cup as I have of winning the London marathon.**❞**

Evening Standard columnist **David Mellor**, 2005

‘England had no direction but more formations than a ballroom dancing team.’

Terry Butcher, unimpressed by England's defeat in Northern Ireland, 2005

‘I honestly believe we have a great chance of winning the World Cup next summer.’

John Terry, 2005

❝Football is a simple game.
Twenty-two men chase a ball for
90 minutes and, in the end,
the Germans win.❞

Gary Lineker

'With both penalties David Beckham snatched at the ball like an adolescent golfer teeing off in front of the clubhouse. The England captain choked.'

Matthew Syed in *The Times* on Beckham's Euro 2004 penalty misses

❛The good news is that Saddam Hussein is facing the death penalty. The bad news is that David Beckham's taking it.**❜**

Anonymous internet joke, 2004